By Elinor Rowe
with
Photos by Kevin White

Note: The book provides information of a general nature and is created and designed for educational and awareness purposes only. If you have concerns and questions about the health of a child, please consult a physician or other healthcare professional.

About Me!

Hi! My name is Ellie!

I was diagnosed with Type One Diabetes in 2016 when I was 8 years old.

The first year after diagnosis was full of the three "C's" challenges, change, and craziness! Eventually, it was easier for me to count carbs, test blood sugars, and dose insulin. A year later, I got an insulin pump with continuous glucose monitor (CGM), which made things even easier!

Diabetes is part of my life, but it fades into the background most days. I love Disney movies, dogs, cats, unicorns, sewing, swimming, art, and reading. My friends inspire me. They encouraged me to write this book. I hope you like it!

I will be donating a portion of proceeds from the book to the Juvenile Diabetes Research Foundation. It's like I always say, "When life hands you lemons, make sugar-free lemonade. And, share it with your friends!"

Alcohol Swabs

Alcohol swabs are very useful! They clean my fingers before I test my blood sugar. And they disinfect my insulin pens before I inject. I use alcohol swabs to wipe off my dose site and keep it free from germs!

 **ag**

My bag carries my diabetic supplies. It holds my insulin, needles, alcohol swabs, insulin pens, and snacks for when I have a low!

It also holds my blood glucose meter, test strips, and glucagon. I always carry the bag for safety.

My bag is always at my side for testing and emergencies!

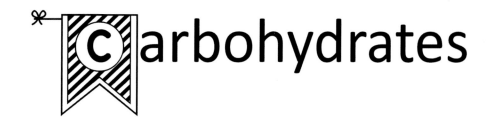arbohydrates

I call these carbs! Carbs are sugars, starches, and fibers. They are in most foods.

My body turns carbs into sugar glucose. This goes into my bloodstream. Then, with help from my insulin, my body uses glucose for energy so I can run, jump, swim, and ride my bike!

People with Type One Diabetes like me have bodies that can't make insulin. So, we inject insulin to safely eat carbs like bread, fruit, and pasta.

My doctor told me to count my carbs so that I know how much insulin to use.

Diabetes

With Type One Diabetes, my body can't make its own insulin. I won't outgrow diabetes. I will have it until there is a cure. I think about diabetes, but I think of lots of other things like school, friends, beach vacations, and my dog, Willow. Diabetes does NOT stop me from having fun!

Eating Healthy

It's important to eat food that is good for me. I like apples, peanut butter, yogurt, cheddar cheese, and milk. I can feel lousy when I eat too many carbs and don't take enough insulin. I try to choose healthy foods and dose right!

Fatigue

Fatigue is another word for tired.

Sometimes, I get very tired when I have high blood sugar or after I've treated a low blood sugar.

When I get up in the night to test my blood sugar, I move like a sloth the next day.

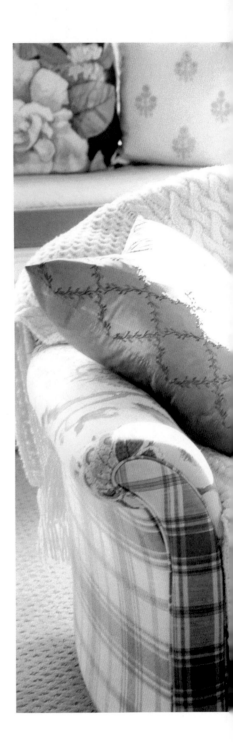

lucagon

Glucagon is a special injection or nasal spray, which is only for emergencies!

It can save my life. If my blood sugar goes super low, my family, teacher, or friends could shake me and if I didn't wake up, then they could call 911 and give me glucagon. If my blood sugar is high, glucagon won't hurt me. If my blood sugar is low, glucagon will wake me up fast. I always carry it in my bag for safety, but I've never had to use it.

Health

I try to stay healthy. When I am sick, my blood sugar runs high. I always wash my hands. I cough into my arm (like a vampire!) to stop spreading germs. I try to avoid people who are sick with colds or the flu. I try to drink water, get lots of rest, and eat healthy foods.

Insulin

Did you know that everyone needs insulin? Since I have diabetes, my body doesn't make its own insulin. I get insulin from a pump or shot. Insulin changes sugar from carbs that I eat into energy that I can use. I ALWAYS keep insulin with me.

unk Food

Junk food isn't good for me, except when I need a fast-acting carb. When my blood sugar is low, I drink juice, eat candy, or take glucose tabs.

Candy is easy to carry in my diabetes bag. It brings up my blood sugar when I need to treat a low.

I don't eat too much, but it sure is tasty!

etones

Ketones appear when I don't have enough insulin in my body to turn sugar into energy. When my blood sugar is high, I test for ketones. I use a test stick that changes color!

Pink shows trace or small ketones. If my test stick is tan or pink, I "drink, drink, drink." Water flushes out ketones. If my ketones are moderate or large, the test stick turns deep purple. When this happens, my family and doctor help me treat my ketones with a dose of insulin. With large ketones, I sometimes go to the hospital for extra care.

Lancet

A lancet or lancing device is a finger poker! First, I wipe my hand with an alcohol swab to clean my finger. Next, I prime the needle of my lancet, pulling back a little lever. I press the button to stick my finger. It's over fast.

Then, I squeeze out a tiny drop of blood. Last, I touch the test strip to the blood drop to check my blood sugar.

eter

A test meter checks my blood sugar.

I test before I eat, exercise, or go to bed. I also test when I feel shaky to see if I am low. I use my lancet to poke my finger, and my blood glucose number appears on the meter.

My meter also stores my blood glucose readings. I always carry my meter with my lancet and test strips in my diabetes bag.

Needle

With diabetes care, I use little needles. These needles are much smaller than the ones I use for sewing.

I use needles for pricking my finger and giving insulin shots. My insulin pump uses a needle at the infusion site.

Needles help me stay healthy and give me insulin. I'm not afraid of them. You shouldn't be either!

Out of Range

My blood glucose range is 70-130. When I go out of range, I don't hit the panic button. If I'm high, I use my pump to get a little more insulin. Sometimes, a grown up helps. I can also drink water and exercise to help lower my blood sugar. When I am low, I have fast-acting carbs like juice, fruit, or candy to raise my blood sugar.

Pump

I have an insulin pump!

It delivers insulin to my body. Before I got my pump, I took shots.
I have an infusion site (where the insulin enters my body). I have tubing to carry the insulin from the pump to my infusion site.

I also have a continuous glucose monitor (CGM) that tells my pump what my blood sugar is. At first, I had a lot to learn about my pump. Now, I am pumped about the technology!

Queasy means feeling sick. When I am queasy, I have a "yuck bucket."

Throwing up is no fun. If I throw up after I dose insulin and eat, then I have insulin in my body but no food. My blood sugar can go low!

I need to get carbs down and keep them down. Sometimes, my mom gives me ginger ale. It makes my tummy feel better and gives me the carbs I need.

When I'm sick, I check for ketones even if my blood sugar is below 240.

If I have large ketones and am throwing up, I go to the emergency room. I can get better faster in the ER. The doctors and nurses help me, so it is not scary.

 # Ratio

I have an insulin-to-carb ratio. This means I need a certain amount of insulin for what I eat.

I use a calculator to help me figure out how much insulin I need for my meal or snack. Fast acting insulin is also called bolus.

Bolus sounds like "bowl us." That makes it easy to remember that I calculate my bolus before I eat.

For example, my insulin-to-carb ratio is 1:15 at lunchtime. I get 1 unit of insulin for every 15 grams of carbohydrates.

I add up all the carbs in my food and divide by 15. Other times of the day, I may need more insulin, so my ratio is 1:10.

Sick

On a sick day, I test for ketones each time I go to the bathroom. I check my blood glucose more often (every 2 hours).

I drink lots of water. I rest to let my body heal.

When I am sick, it takes time to bounce back. I must be fever free without medicine for 24 hours before I go back to school.

My mom takes good care of me. Snuggling, sleeping, reading, and watching my favorite movies help on sick days.

Transmitting

My mom uploads the numbers from my test meter onto the computer. We send the blood glucose readings to my doctor. My doctor gets a bigger and better picture of my blood glucose numbers over time.

Urine

Urine means pee. Ha! Ha! Ha!

Remember ketones? I test for ketones with my urine.

I pee on keto sticks to test for ketones. When the sticks turn different colors, that means the ketones are too large.

But it's okay. I know what to do!

Very High

When my blood glucose level is VERY high, I feel mad and tired at the same time. I check for ketones if my blood glucose is above 240. I may need extra insulin to get my blood sugar back in range and/or treat ketones. I drink extra water. If I don't have moderate or large ketones, I can also exercise to lower my blood glucose.

Water

Water is refreshing and cool. It's important, too! Water helps me lower blood sugar and flush out ketones. It is a healthy drink and a good choice.

-tremely Low

Arrrrrrrgggghhhhhhhh! Why the screaming? Well, eXtremely low blood sugars can be very dangerous.

Family, teachers, and friends know the signs of an extreme low and how to help. When I'm low, I feel shaky. But, if I go extremely low, I may not know it. I might act in a different way. I could even pass out.

If I ever pass out from a low blood sugar, people around me call 911 and give glucagon. I can usually catch and treat a low.

When I am low (below 70), I eat or drink a fast-acting carb. I wait 15 minutes. I test my blood glucose again. I repeat 15 carbs with 15 minutes between tests until I am back in range (above 70).

 **Young**

Y is for young people with diabetes.

I'm not alone! We're not alone! Close to 200,000 Americans under age 20 have Type One Diabetes.

People may not immediately know I have diabetes. I'm busy doing my thing—playing, going to school, crafting, worshipping, singing, and living my life.

Type One Diabetes isn't like a getting a cold or having the flu. No one can catch it or get rid of Type One with what they eat or how much they move. My pancreas doesn't work, but doctors know how to help. Scientists work each day on new medical devices and look for a cure.

Zany

We made it to the end of the alphabet and the end of the book!

Life with Type One Diabetes can be zany and crazy!

I think about testing, dosing, and always carrying supplies. But I still do the fun things I did before diabetes.

With the same strength that diabetes takes, I can do things that I love like writing this book!

What if when you grow up, you help people with diabetes or even cure it! Just imagine!

It's zany but 100% possible... just like life with diabetes!

Additional Resources

American Diabetes Association

www.diabetes.org

1.800.DIABETES (342.2383)

Mission: To prevent and cure diabetes and to improve the lives of all people affected by diabetes.

Children with Diabetes

www.childrenwithdiabetes.com

Mission: Children with Diabetes focuses on care today, so we are ready for a cure tomorrow.

Diabetes Patient Advocacy Coalition (DPAC)

www.diabetespac.org

The Diabetes Patient Advocacy Coalition (DPAC) is an alliance of people with diabetes, caregivers, patient advocates, health professionals, disease organizations and companies working collaboratively to promote and support public policy initiatives to improve the health of people with diabetes.

Juvenile Diabetes Research Foundation

www.jdrf.org

800.533.CURE (2873)

Improving lives today and tomorrow by accelerating life-changing breakthroughs to cure, prevent and treat T1D and its complications.

Kids with Courage

www.kidswithcourage.org

Courage@kidswithcourage.org

816.478.0253

Providing opportunities that empower, educate, and create positive outcomes in the lives of children, young people, and families whose life-long journey includes battling Type 1 Diabetes.

 **A**cknowledgements

Dedication
**To my Nana & Grandpa "Pa" (Shirlee &
Roy Nichols) with all my love**

Thank you to my good friends for praying
for me, learning about diabetes, and
treating me the same after my diagnosis.

Thank you to Dr. Karen Hearty at Pediatric
Associates and to Children's Mercy
Hospital in Kansas City for caring for me.

Thank you to all my wonderful teachers at
Springfield Lutheran School. Special
thanks to Mrs. Sarah Tessaro for helping
me from the very start. Thank you to Ms.
Amanda Cole for learning about my
insulin pump alongside me. And, thank
you for assigning fourth graders to write a
primer. (Spoiler alert: It became this
book!)

My mom writes a blog about family life
with Type One Diabetes, The Helpful
Type. She helps me every day. Mom and
Dado, thank you both for EVERYTHING. I
love you!

And to all of you: Thanks for reading!

Made in the USA
Middletown, DE
09 December 2020